PILGRIMAGE TO DHARAMSALA AND OTHER POEMS

by

Marion L. Matics

Drawings by the author

PILGRIMAGE TO DHARAMSALA AND OTHER POEMS

by

MARION L. MATICS, Ph.D.

Design: K.I. Matics
© 1985 by Marion L. Matics, all rights reserved.

Printed in Thailand
by Craftsman Press,
487/42 Soi Wattanasilp,
Bangkok, Thailand.

ISBN 974–8495–04–3

Published by White Lotus Co. Ltd.,
16 Soi 47 Sukhumvit,
Bangkok 10110, Thailand.
Tel: 392-7449
Telex: 82094 ANDE TH

TO

GESHÉ WANGYAL

CONTENTS

INTRODUCTION

"Pilgrimage to Dharamsala" means to convey something of the mood of those early days after March 1959 when the Dalai Lama and hosts of Tibetan refugees were forced to flee from their country and to seek refuge wherever they could find it. World opinion had much to say, all slanted to predictable political ends, but none cared to intervene, so once again might made right. The pleasant young man who had ruled this isolated and medieval kingdom was given shelter by the Government of India on the southwest border of the Himalayas in the beautiful hill town of Dharamsala. Other refugees found shelter as best they could. The invaders assumed political and economic power, systematically destroyed the institutions of the old culture, brutally persecuted the people's religion, tortured and massacred dissidents. All was peaceful. All was quiet.

After a time of shock and stupor life began again for the refugees. Many visitors with varying interests ranging from curiosity to a search for truth began to visit Dharamsala and brought back reports of the renewal and intense vitality of Buddhist culture found there and in other refugee centers. Then in September 1960 His Holiness the Dalai Lama — until then, the recluse of Dharamsala, appeared on the Himalayan slopes before thousands of his homeless followers, spoke kind words to encourage them, and prayed for his country, and for its invaders as well, in a prayer which is a classic of religious devotion. Parts of this prayer, beautifully translated by Thutop Tulku and Freda Bedi, are included in this work. It is a case again of "Father, forgive them; for they know not what they do."

Nonetheless, questions must rise in the mind of the sympathic Westerner, especially anyone historically minded who remembers that before its conversion to the gentle religion of Buddhism the Tibetans demanded and received tribute from Imperial China, and that the Chinese Emperors sometimes encouraged the spread of this religion among subject peoples to render them harmless. One remembers also the tedious and endless obligation imposed upon Tibet by its geographical location to balance political interests between China and various Indian kingdoms — superpowers of their day, all of which can be misinterpreted and twisted by the modern propagandist who ends up with the legal fiction that "Tibet is part of

China." No wonder the Tibetans sought isolation and preferred to cultivate religion; but there will always be a question if force would have been better?

The callousness of foreign powers eager to accept the convenient legal fiction of the day also added to the tragedy of "the land of lost content" (following Noel Barber) and this, too, is something to ponder. The whole tragedy is recorded in official documents gathered in "Tibet in the United Nations: 1950—1961" published in New Delhi by the Bureau of the Dalai Lama. The atrocities in the poem (besides the basic atrocity of the invasion and the suppression of an ancient culture and a beautiful religion) are taken directly from the testimony of refugees related in "Tibet and the Chinese People's Republic: A Report to the International Commission of Jurists by its Legal Inquiry Committee on Tibet" published by the International Commission of Jurists, Geneva, 1960. The conscience of the world is burdened by many such seemingly lost causes and by the apparently endless suffering of the innocent at the hands of the violent and the greedy. Will mankind ever grow up enough to learn the ways of peace? One wonders, one doubts, one hopes.

Of course we all know that Tibet was primitive, medieval, and from the point of view of science and technology, a backward place indeed. And we know that its social structure was certainly not perfect — but, then, were its invaders perfect? or is any people or place? And we know, too, the priorities of Tibet lay in good humor, kindliness, gentleness, a sense of transiency and an extraordinarily optimistic view of ultimate reality. Of all the people of the twentieth century they, as a group, were the most devoted to spiritual pursuits and so the world punished them. An irony? or just what we should expect?

Lama Govinda put the matter succinctly as a symbolic struggle between two worlds: a "struggle between spiritual freedom and material power, between the wisdom of the heart and the knowledge of the brain, between the dignity of the human individual and the herd-instinct of the mass, between the faith in the higher destiny of man through inner development and the belief in material prosperity through an ever-increasing production of goods." In the short run materialism and brute force generally prevail but the glorious dharma-megha — the cloud of ultimate law, remains forever beyond our reach, untouched, pure, radiant and beckoning. Somehow gentleness is repeatedly destroyed, but never dies. Somehow the quest for the ultimate is forever ridiculed and debased, but always rises again — somehow, somewhere, sometime. Perhaps it just cannot be our true nature to be satisfied with violence, greed, and death.

Other poems in the collection deal with somewhat similar themes — mostly Buddhist in imagery, in less politically disturbing context.

Marion L. Matics
Staten Island, New York
U.S.A

Protector

1

THE SACRED SOIL

The sacred soil is all the same. The nature of rocks is all the same. All soil is sacred or none is sacred. It does not end its sacredness because a boundary line upon a map is drawn. How can one return to a place called "home" when one is here at home? These arbitrary lines upon a map cause such disaster and always pushing out as if somehow a bigger country was the best. People are all the same and would roam across all boundaries as forest animals from wood to wood, but for such fancies as a country or a place. No one divides the sea, the wind, the sky, and if the land is cut and named and holy war proclaimed, the birds do not know why, animals do not know why, the rain and drifting mist do not know why, and only people claim to know. They claim to understand the lines upon the map and why soil here is more sacred than soil there. If the stars are watching, or the creatures of the sky, they too must wonder that men should die for this.

2

PILGRIMAGE TO DHARAMSALA
AN INTERVIEW WITH HIS HOLINESS
TENZIN GYATSHO, THE 14th DALAI LAMA OF TIBET

The mists ceaseless in the mountains and some kind of Oriental
Pine—whatever it might be, whatever anything might be—
With other tall and quiet trees forever moist. A crystal drop
Hangs beneath the bough and leaf, sedately slides along
The clustered needles and the twig, rests upon the moss and fern.
Towering ghostly peaks of green imagine they are mountain
Shapes, emerge and watch, then drift directionless until again
The mist is darkened by the rain. They are—or they are not—
Or something in between, or not—first rank of Himalayan grandeur
Little brothers of a clan majestically at ease in ice and splendor
Trespassing on the border. "What is it here in the dry season?"
"Beautiful," said the young monk. "Really very nice, but now. . . ."
He wiped the dampness from his brow, his dark red cloak
Was damp, his hair a glistening sheen. Occasionally the sun
Bursting, and the joyous azure ocean of a tropic zone luminous
With cloud dragons playful as puppies rearing, leaping, biting,
Assuming fantastic shapes in brilliant light dancing gave
An unreal sense to the reality of the amorphous grey and
Shifting mist. Shapes appear and disappear, and one remarks
"That was a man, and that another dragon—I mean, a cloud. . . . . . .
That was a laughing girl—gazing quietly amused—a real Tibetan
Beauty." Her eyes an undiscovered gem from some distant
Himalayan mine where dark stones gleam. Her immediate implication
A kind of child's philosophy. The incarnate life is after all
A pleasant game and almost anything a joke and cause
For friendly laughing. But before recognition she is lost
In the family of the nameless, and a twinge of regret this

3

Damp moss-covered stone where one sits uncomfortable
Shivers beneath a large umbrella. Anyway looking out wondering
At the village. An old woman in a small dark store
Sells turquoise beads to a stranger. Her broad expressive features
Squint to hide sun drenched baked dried centuries of desert
And life among the golden horde restlessly shifting
From rock to rock and bouncing back from one mountain
Range to still another in the enormous fecund bowl
Of Asia. Even the message of the Enlightened One did not put
A stop to all that fidgeting, but only to the violence simply
For a moment. In the center of the mist stands some semblance
Of a town—an open space, a chorten with prayer wheels
Suitably placed for circumambulation—and a small bazaar
Some cave-like stores with friendly people dissolving in
And drifting out and acting somewhat three-dimensional
Anachronistic in this land of cloud and rain. On the lower
Slope a trace of mountain road vertical ribbon crumpling
In the hands of the mountain god, waterfall cascading
Down to past and lesser lives. And on the upper side a path
Suggests a walk around a little hill. And not too far away
A temple. . .and beyond that temple the ocean of the highest peaks
and then, Tibet. . . .

Chorten at Dharamsala

THE CHORTEN

This chorten, sepulchre white yet strangely cheerful, while long
    white streamers hung from upright poles quite gaily flutter
Sanskrit prayers in all directions. A small white mountain solid in
    grey haze, an image of a universe, the world mountain
Written in a tiny script, legible at a glance, yet almost too difficult
    to learn. No problem now, for the town's folk
Walk on the left hand side following the course of that legendary sun
    which so they say exists behind the mist, above the mountains
On the other side of daily thick and hovering sky which darkly
    threatens rain more comfortable. The arm outstretched
To reach the wheel of prayer, the fingers grasp the metal cylinder,
    a push of palm sends it spinning animate. *Oṁ, maṇi padme,
    hūṁ.*
And the prayers bright firecracker sputter on muttering lips and
    murmuring eyes—except the ones which are terribly broken.
It is all quite casual. Even the animals walk by habit on
    the proper side in the Tibet that used to be. (That used to be
Solid as a world mountain peaceful in a raging sea of universal
    passion.) But whatever is in the chorten is untouched—the
    relic of radiant
Saints, the bone or hair or fingernail which heals upon the touch, the
    palm-leaf fragment of the Buddha's word. Such vibrations of
    subtile matter—
Or is it thought? resound within the solid upside bell and toll
    the blessings of the day   His great legs crossed, giant feet
In lotus posture, lion chest uplifted, with hands peaceful
    mudrā clad, and head erect and eyes far-seeing inward:
The Buddha is the chorten, or so it seems to floating Nāgas—
    or maybe levitating saints, who happen piercingly to glance
Clairvoyant through the fog, the human heart, and other kinds of
    mist.

THE PORCH

On the other side of the hill, surrounded by aforementioned tiers of
　　higher mountains and other insubstantial shapes of cloud
Is an open space between the temple and some low and rambling
　　conversation in a Western style,
More or less. Sad Indian guards saunter fitfully with precision less
　　than military and rather shuffling pleasant
And the secret service at his desk upon the open porch makes a few
　　pertinent remarks. I sign my name. Give address and age,
State nationality; but purpose of the visit—that is hard to say—
　　certainly not to sell and not to buy, not exactly visit
And not to laugh, exactly. Well, we can let the purpose go, while
　　I struggle to take galoshes off. No, I have no grenades.
I am not carrying firearms or dynamite. I have no weapons and
　　no bomb ticks in my Pan Am bag. No, curiosity is
Not the purpose—in a way, that is not the purpose—tourism is too
　　undignified a word for a statement of metaphysical purpose.
I can swear that no instruments of nuclear fission are concealed
　　about my person: but what then, O Lama, is a person?
And I have no intention, so I think, to explode the world: but what
　　is an I? and what is a world? and could I weeping wish to make
　　it more inflated?
Or blown down? Or dissolved like a cube of sugar in the
　　drinking water of some Upanishadic sage? No matter, I will
　　fold my umbrella,
Wait, rearrange my raincoat on my arm, and quietly sit looking out.
　　Looking out at the openness and the wind
Nudging the pine trees gently, here and there to serve an artistic
　　Purpose. Looking out at the soft grey mist drifting

Between the mountain peaks and above the high places and down
   the pass towards the valley. One-pointed looking out
To the temple rising bravely beyond the open space and past that
   hill which hides the village where Tibetans weave
Their rugs, sell blue beads, circumambulate the chorten, and have a
   family. What manner of hospitality is this bureaucratic
   welcome—
No Tibetan tea, but only conversation! The emptiness between
   the house and temple catches one's eye and again I observe
The openness. Beyond the village a rock road writhes and rages.
   While on the Indian plains the masses surge below, beat
   against the cliffs and fall in surf and foam. And beyond that,
   other seas. . . .
And still beyond—a few miles backwards past the border—those
   passion fields where hungry ghosts devour themselves with no
   suspicion that anything at all can be
Beyond the selfish limitations of a fear-filled day! History turns and
   twists and writhes phenomenal. So blood pools proudly
   swirl. . . .
Then drink and bathe; unless this morbid lack of thought offends,
   and one prefers the looking out, preferably in another far
   direction to another
World! Two monks amble across the courtyard, holding umbrellas
   above red cloaks, disappear within some trees, and the
   openness
Is left. Looking out from the Lama's porch—a suggestion of a meaning and a message. And then my lack of name is called.

THE MONK

A funny thing happened on the way to the Dalai Lama
    hard to believe and maybe human stupid
On my part, but comic anyway. In the waiting room
    a monk came in and nodded yellow
Robed and sat upon the sofa. No introduction. No howdy-do.
    No pleasant talk about the weather being damp
How it's nicer here in summer, then you see the mountains
    fine, and you should come in another season
Or another life. None of that. But plop upon the sofa
    in the lotus posture, chest up-lifted, rhythmic
Breathing, eyes are closed in meditation. Rather odd
    behavior in a Western room for an Oriental
Image of a man. The silence so embarassing that a shriek
    or two would clear the air. The restless
Monk shifts position, looks suspicious, retreats beyond the silence.
    Is this the Dalai Lama?
It looks like him, but Orientals tend to look alike
    and Chinese food simply does not stay with one—
You're hungry right away, and other witty sayings. . . .
    He is the age, and the horn rimmed glasses
And the royal presence. What is protocol? Should I
    speak first, be still, or scream, or meditate
To keep him company? It is the Dalai Lama!
    Who else these days is golden, still and royal?
So I fidget, wondering what to do or say or think
    while the room fills with such silence
That I cannot breathe. The Dalai Lama is not hospitable
    to act this way. It is up to him to speak

Not I—the secret words of wisdom, if they exist,

for he is supposed to be somehow mysterious—

Not me, although I feel mysterious, but mostly now

uncomfortable. Or course the monk was someone

Unexpected, waiting his turn eccentric, just like me,

and finally spoke. "It's nicer here in summer,

Not this ocean filled with rain." "So the summer is clear. . . ."

I bristled dog-teeth snarling conversational.

"What's the matter

With now. Now is the accepted time. Now is the day of salvation"

"That's good Buddhism," said the monk

And laughed. Later I heard that in the small hotel

he gave the hippies quite a start, meditating unexpected

With no warning. Lobbies were not safe. Neither the top

of the stairs, nor the end of the hall. He carried silence

Wherever he went, and nothing is more dangerous—

All of a sudden, someone sitting in meditation,

peace and still!

His Holiness was jibber-jabber friendly. Avalokitésvara and Bodhisattva like—teeth and eyes and ears and talking—in another Western
room. Pausing now and then to let the secretary reach between the
gaps of English and Tibetan—such curious modes for pointing out
a lack of anything at all except the Higher Nature. A red robed
Lama— his glasses rimmed in dark, the Ocean of Virtues was most
alert, competent, so very puzzling and kind. While reaching out the
secretary another gentle monk with unpronounceable name and
transcendental gesture made the introduction for this particular time
and place: Greetings again and of course it is nice to meet anyone
especially from anywhere. And on my part—especially a child who
knew the rosary of a former version of a Dalai Lama, his possessions,
and his secrets—while somewhere the incarnate spirit of compassion
breathed another blessing to the world. Since we do not speak of
"self" there is and there is not a Dalai Lama, but a kind of spirit
shared; although a leering shadow becomes a grinning form and on
each porcelain image of compassion lays his heavy fist. When
smashing hard at will pieces shattered on the floor resound. Nothing
mended ever is the same. Far the Potala, the Dalai Lama now in
temporary residence, they say, (like the Aremenians) on the fringe
of mountains is at home.

All

those documents and the claim of suzerainty over Tibet in 1907.
Ages passed before 1907. But not as many as now perhaps. And
anyway, the 1907 Convention was between Great Britain and
Russia then dickering about some real estate they wanted. "It may
be pointed out that Tibet was not a party to that Convention and
was in no way bound. . . . The Tibetan Government calls on the

The Dalai Lama

United Nations for help. . . ." What is that? it calls for what? who
calls? Ridiculous!
"The delegation of the Soviet Union objects to
the inclusion in the agenda of the so-called
                        Question. . . .

                    It is not designed to improve
the international situation or relations among the States. . . ." Not
designed at all, this so-called question. And Tibet appeals again. . . .
appeals again. . . .appeals again. . . .appeals again. . . .But the case is
settled: Before 1952 one or two Chinese traders lived in Lhasa, and
a few Chinese Tibetans. . . . Sound of the falling gavel. But Tibet
still calls. Beneath an earthquake avalanche of argument, its mouth
is stuffed with paper. Yet calls to the U.N. calls to the U.N. calls to
the U.N. calls to the U.N. about
                    the so-called

                    what was the question?
Back home they are sleeping beyond a dateline change of time and
inclination, yet the compassion of all the Buddhas, *Oṁ. mani padme,
hūṁ. Hrīḥ,* splits into a thousand pieces at the sight of suffering in
the six directions questioning.

AVALOKITEŚVARA

He could be a Buddha if he wished with a wish beyond desire.
He is a Mahābodhisattva—isn't everyone? but for compassion's
Sake he acts. When a thousand young men in a distant world vowed
    to achieve Enlightenment, Avalokiteśvara paused
And made the incredible Vow—to care what happens
    to another living creature! To care about the gods in restless
Splendour—to really care that the antigods should find surcease
    of hate—and hungry ghosts be given food and drink—
And the tormented hells be filled with blessing. No righteousness,
    no justice here, no moral indignation, lip smacking pride
That they deserve exactly what they karmic get. And men—
    even these, are treated with the love reserved for pets.
Praised by animals and men, by gods and ghosts and anti-
    gods and things in hell so deep their feelers barely touch
The lower scab of bottom slime: Avalokiteśvara radiates his pure
    blessing of good will without restraint
And kindness without price. Looking out at passion burn
    and hatred writhe and the sloth of caring vacuum slight
Or not at all what happens: the Mahābodhisattva climbs
    the ladder of the six directions, stumbling, falling—
Then descends and harkens to the cries above so pitiful
    and reaching up is called below, and wearisome
He strikes to touch an Ego pain and neal with soothing
    quiet wisdom. Looking down from some far city of the gods
Past the world of ghosts and men, and other realms mentionable
    only when one weeps, he observed hell filling faster
Than even he could empty it, and the six directions
    caught in the entanglements of unresisted sorrow.

Everywhere he looked was birth and death, sickness,
   old age, aversion, pride, ego, youth, and sorrow everywhere
Like a pomegranate splitting his head broken open and shattering
   pain while the body flies into a thousand trembling pieces.
When the Buddhas made him whole again in such a way
   that he could stand before the sorrow, his thousand arms
Could reach compassionate, every head observe a better path
   for those who need, with Vajrapāṇi power to. help,
And the head of Amitābha on the top to speak a higher
   Blessing. A thousand arms and eleven heads of love
And from his grateful eye the falling tear who became
   the goddess Tārā. *Oṁ, maṇi padme, hūṁ, Hrīḥ!*
Hail to the bearer of the Lotus and the Jewel, the spirit
   in the heart of true compassion wherever this may be!

FIRST QUESTION

Wherever this may be, and not least in aspiration upon the throne
Of old Tibet.   The interview against a background quite exotic
As kindness—no less bizarre than caring for another creature—
Quite as gaudy as one Inconceivable which is and yet is
Not in any human terms.
                          Somewhat hesitant the question:
What Karma—assuming Karma, moral cause and sure effect
Taken for granted for the argument at least—what could explain
This particular suffering of Tibetan people?   What did they do
That was so bad?   Good Karma exhausted?   used up and limp?
Or bad Karma of the outside world?   What merits this?
Were you so evil that you had to be destroyed?   And those laughing
People clawing at the mountains with mind and body chained?
Why?   and where is justice?   that is first of all the questions
And not meaning to offend, what happens to the theories?

There was this fat refugee brought naked to the village—
not so bad, although he had enough to eat and guilty—
prodded with bayonets to walk the faster.   Grinning soldiers
tie him to a tree with raw wounds dripping. Not many
trees in old Tibet, but they say the scenery is unsurpassed;
while mineral resources, they are superb.
A lot to buy and sell and
where were we?   Oh, yes,
                          Tied to the tree accused of

Cruelty.   The good-natured soldiers shout the charges in his eyes
and teeth, inviting all Tibet to join a joyful litany of accusation:
But no Tibetan speaks.   Again, the kindly comrade officer
in charge issues the hospitable invitation.

                              Beat the man,

He is free and may be beaten! But these days people are so
ungrateful that of all that Tibetan village no surly individual
comes to prove his liberation. Not a miserable Tibetan will
lift the stick or chain or sword. And the slobbering nude
cries out flesh folds quivering and stomach distended
Asking to be shot. Begging to be shot rather than be tortured.
The Motherland cannot stand this breach of etiquette and peace.
So his lips are sliced off to stop the begging.
                                        So kindly Chinese
do the beating and he takes eight days to die. . . . A karmic
Problem?. . . .
Memories of Tibet by the hundreds of witnesses escaped
Ghost-like haunt the pages of unread legal books. Wangtok—
nobody much, one of hordes of once breathing Orientals and a
Problem. He would not tell the secret place of hidden treasure
So "beaten with sticks, poured over with boiling water, slung up
by his big toes
              and thumbs,
                        and cooked over a fire
                                        to tell

Where his treasure is hidden." But this reactionary cannot
Screaming tell, because he has no fortune. A red-hot
copper nail hammered in his forehead finally shuts him up.

The monks imprisoned without food so they can prove
the power of religion. The head Lama exquisitely smothered,
one more buried breathing.   The monks driven from the temple to
a prostitute and marriage bed. Loving bayonets assist the ice-eyed
witnesses who in the corner smirk. And the images once sacred
Smashed in lamasery barracks for the soldiers. Little
families smashed accusing one another, starving, maimed,
and children sent to China. "Prayer books are thrown in the streets
and burned. The drums and cymbals broken." Just history.
Racial genocide and cultural murder is quite simple
and an unconvincing legal fiction gives us reason to forget. . . .

    Our mothers calling in the weeping night
    Our fathers groping at the darkened door
    While starved within and starved without
    Small children are aborted from their families
    To be taught by bullhorn and loudspeaker
    In the romantic city of Peking. . . . bones
    And blood and viscera spilled. . . . minds drip
    With the sacred places made most foul
    And place names changed for a whole
    New population. The monks dispersed or dead
    Where the Buddha image stood but now
    A brand new flag of Empire. The day
    Of slogans greets the dawn. The colonists return.
    In true equality each man is now his own war-
    Lord. . . .at least to that warlord who stands below.

Forget. . .forget. . .forget. . . . It is only a little incident
In history. Others were not worse, but larger.
No need to be excited. . . . In the spider's web it does not
Pay to look too closely. We are hurt by what we do not know.

Anyway, we sit peacefully discussing Karma, and I wait
All this surgery subconscious for the answer. Thus and
So, says the Dalai Lama, every action does cause an effect
And causes are accumulated by the whole person himself.
The cosmic law invades the pleasant room and the mountains
Bow before an inexorable majesty outside the window
And within. On a superficial level, Tibetans seem to be
A religious people, but cause and effect is not limited
To one lifetime only. Who can trace causation? all
The causes of an act? Only a Buddha and everyone suffers causes
In accumulation. Lifetime after lifetime giant causes cluster
and mountain-like they rise as shadows of the sun. So
Tibetans suffer from cause heaped up in many previous
Lives. Some, too, are not inwardly religious, however
Outward practising. The exterior may look religious, but
Those people are worse than the unbelievers. So he spoke,
Insofar as one could catch the meaning. Clear, crisp,
Icy and severe: but not unkind. Only relentlessly descriptive.
It seemed almost as if what happened could to any people happen,
But like original sin strikes most painfully the infant vulnerable
And innocent—although none are innocent. He did not bother
To excuse Tibetans or to blame another or reinterpret karmic law.
Curious! He might have said something to explain something away
To justify the orphans in the village down below in mist.

SECOND QUESTION

The special help of skillful means and the winds of spiritual force,
    beating as two wings of a bird in the blue void
Of space, "winging one's way to Buddhahood," he had said; and so
    the question was not inappropriate regarding violence.
"After the tragic results of its practise in Tibet, is non-violence
    really justified? Why did it work in India and not in Tibet?"
Always why? Memories of a holy crank, an old man saint, a sage
    who never youthful sang but strictly vegetarian, walking
With a stick and several billion people spindle legged in diapers,
    and through his glasses grinning down the walls of ancient
Prisons, while nice young men with British crispness shuffle foot to
    foot, toying with their excellent firearms and musing
What to do? Brahmins and British both came toppling down before
    that onslaught of absurdity too humorous for either caste or
Empire Building. And no matter what, he still taught love. Never
    gloating. Not unkind. As if he were a Dalai Lama arms
    outstretched.
But in Tibet the only foreign policy was that polite request peculiar—
    that they be left alone. The Himalayas were their walls
With deserts to the north and east. The melancholy winds now laden
    with a lifting voice of protest and the sands so heavy moist
Stale blooded testify their innocence. If they did not want
    the wheel—the prison hours nine to five, appetite machines
who devour cannibal all they seek to serve, the routine dissent
    and shoulder clawing, with refinements chromium and neon
    shiny of
Happy hour and battlefield. They wanted not to want. . . .

20

And when the legal fiction descended south, fully armed
with ugly words (and not to mention guns) to fill the air
with shouts against tranquility, and violence
Calling: they turned the other cheek as best they could—
with about the same result as Jesus Christ.
"From the Buddhist point of view," said the Ocean of Virtues,
"even for national causes non-violence is the method
To be emphasized." He elucidated no further the distinction
between India and Tibet. "And when we talk about religion
Which is personal and quite private, non-violence is the law."
He shrugged his shoulders. "There is a difference between
The individual and the nation as a whole." He preferred to talk
no more, it seemed, of tigers gnawing at the broken back
chewing at the spurting vein.
The nation always problematic
in a rocky corner
Ah, but the Dharma green and a singing mountain
spring. . . .

THIRD QUESTION

Trying again with Western zeal, "For the people of China what hope
    is there to rise above the present standard? The lack of
    standard? Is there hope, I mean, to rise above materialism
    ever?"
"Of course. They cannot remain there where they are." The sun
    flecked shadows outside listen, but hear no more. He did not
    explain why they cannot remain exactly where they are—or
    worse changed, according to the law of change—icosahedran-
    like multiplied to infinity for the worse—a serpent headed
    hell and fertile.
He did not say "the Buddha nature," for that would be the usage
    of another school. Even "a Divine Image re-asserting," or
    "a child of God" or "Christ within"—that would do, but that
    is another universe of thought, besides another school.
His optimism church bells chiming like Tibetan growling horns
    before a temple. The Bodhisattva's duty is good will to
    hungry teeth and daggers.
A waterfall of silence between the towering greens of mountain mist
    fills the little room, and in the hush we tiptoe on to still
    important
                    Questions. . . .

FOURTH QUESTION

They are always praying, these red clothed monks, for somebody
or someone else. And even the Dalai Lama before thousands
chanted a prayer for Tibet and China, too. Yes, for China:
since it is not in Avalokiteśvara to renege after once com-
mitted to a course of universal kindness.
So sneaky--like the question came of intercessory prayer, and how
could this be possible in a religion of self-help?
An animal suffering by the road
A child in tears
A man or woman torn by pain
What then?
What does one say to oneself? to God? or any Ultimate Power
handy?
Reach down and help
This mangled ball of fur
This broken bird or man
Twisted out of shape in immemorial quivering patterns.
Reach down. . . .Touch. . . .and soothe. . . . .Damn it,
where's your sacred heart?
Oṁ, maṇi padme, hūṁ — in one interpretation is a prayer for every
living creature that it may find release. And it does not have
to be much living.
Thus through the realms of pain in six directions strides the Bodhisattva. Buzzing thick a wing which insects hear in stinking
garbage dumps of old Benares. Rustling of a thousand leaves
in shadows where deer and antelope abruptly start. Eyes
upon the outstretched palm by day. A nighttime soft and
gliding presence past the nervous terror. Gentle touch upon
some accidental blood and down the sterile corridors to the

23

crowded funeral pyre. Mercy is not just in hell nor in the
jungle twilight.

Anyway, said His Holiness, not so smiling now, no teeth. "Generally
everything which happens is dependent upon ourselves. One
person praying for another has no

Effect." A saddening statement, generally, perhaps. But he con-
tinued about special circumstances and the case of two persons
who specifically related in past lives lived again, and then, a
prayer on behalf of another may have an effect. Maybe.
Maybe may have an effect.

But if it were possible to help another very much there is the Buddha. If there were psychic effect we would not suffer. "There
would be no reason why we should suffer because there is the
Buddha." Not

To mention others, I suppose. Anyway, the Buddha or another or
the same would pray and effect would follow fast and soothing.

Of course some kind of effect does follow anything and every prayer
does something good for someone else somehow. So I thought
But the Ocean of Virtues stressed the independent.

"There must be self-help. We must always think of others: this is
the Mahayana doctrine, but the main goal for them is wisdom.
To get rid of ignorance, to know—That they may have something good."

Indeed, the right path, the teaching, and the knowledge. The
Buddha path across the lotus pond from one green pad a
faltering step across the muddy waters to another blossom
white glistening against the green and darkness. . . .

So prayer helps indirectly in the Bodhisattva's case. Who desires
only to desire to help another and is able to show the proper
way,

He is the flower crushed.

Oh, meditate on *bodhicitta,* the Enlighten-
ment-aspiring consciousness—that bridge across the chasm of
one phenomenal false self which gives facility to such a cross-
ing: the Lama puts us straight on that.
But from the other bank: Who has not had specific relationship
with all infinity of others? The universe of past lives touches
all. And overlaps. Praying is self-help, if there is no self who
is not somehow another. The web vibrates at the slightest
touch. The mind creates. And prays.
One of the symbols of the Buddha was the rain now falling
—the Raincloud of Virtue, as darkening now and windows
Drenched and crying. Splashes on the concrete path intense
with bongo rhythm, a drum upon the roof.
Exhilaration of the bursting udder, while the room is shadow real.
As the Buddha said during another rainy season, O ye monks:
Some men are a drought and where they walk is desert dry
—a stone on which to stumble, a thirsting famine
and a stifling
Sun, a parched and cracking mouth, a splitting lip, and panting
—or words to that effect. And other men are local rains
—the comfortable split level, our family seated at the T.V. hearth.
Here and now face value shields the Now.
Involving anguish; nothing wrong with children and being nice to
Mother, and in the freezer frozen slabs of duty—
So the Buddha said, but not exactly. Ah, yes, nothing really wrong;
and yet the Arhat is a monsoon swollen
Punctured drenching kindness. The Bodhisattva rain falls on healthy
corpse and decaying poor corpse killer
Without distinction, as far as kindness is concerned, admitting no
distinction than universal pathos cutting:
And so a kind of prayer is possible by identification with while still
without the fallen bird or monkey in the snare.

"As a monkey ! ! !"

FIFTH QUESTION

"As a monkey faring through the jungle and wood catches
Hold of a bough and, having let it go, takes hold of another,"
In the way that five "heaps" posture as a man. By consciousness
Played upon, strings pulled, manipulated one to five
Into this or that transformation, dissolving fast enough
To reappear in other form and feeling different in the way
That causes past and future are perceived and calculated
By what they call the mind: another question and no more play.

In regard, dear Sir, to the non-self doctrine, what is enlightened
        if there is no self? In a state of selfless Enlightenment
Does any abiding individuality remain? Something must be
        enlightened. . . . I mean to say, how otherwise? I guess?
This inadequate vocabulary—as if any words were good—
A filament of the problem's root. All words are most misleading
Now or at any other time, although perhaps some vocabularies
Suit a moment. Śūnyatā, for example, to take a word—
Considering at random Void or Emptiness—it just happened
To be on one's mind at the moment—are terms perhaps
More fit and proper for another time or maybe not. How
To describe the inner nature?—if inner nature is permitted
As a term—Plenum, Fullness, All, and Everything. Why not
Oṁ? A point of consciousness beyond conceiving is the Lotus
Jewel. Conundrum laughing, or some pathetic beautiful joke
Beyond awakening. I mean to say, do I make myself quite
        Clear. . . .

27

The Dalai Lama laughed very seriously. As the monsoon
Bursting—as they say he does in frequent interviews
When a passing question catches quick the eye—to intensely
Lecture on a theme much like a secret passage through the walls
Of understanding. It is humorous and solemn really,
But no matter(here I paraphrase), something is enlightened.

"What is the Divine Gloom?" asked Dionysius. . . .
    "Unto this Darkness which is beyond Light we pray
that we may come. . . ." Oh, vision beyond sight!
    Oh, knowledge beyond knowing! Perception beyond
perceiving to a Darkness hidden by all the light
    of existent things, things, things, things, things.

Perhaps better put, no self exists which by itself exists
Or thing exists which in itself is not related in a friendly
Way to every other thing. Not only a poor sad self in vacuum
Tube shivering does not *not* exist without dependence, so every
Thing and even now the Buddha is dependent or he would not be
In any sense. After salvation, still there is no thing and
Something is enlightened. The Buddha is enlightened. An individual
Still, but with no self-existence—no independent self—no
Absolute beyond Ineffable. Everything is relative, even
The Absolute depends upon the relative to be Absolute. Thus and
So the Buddha still is somewhat relative and exists himself in
Relativity, except that he shares the Absolute in another way
Than ordinary. . . . But to really understand all Dharma is to be
A Buddha. (The last remark is mine. Take it absolute or relative
        with Tibetan tea.)

Meditation anyway is better than philosophy. It is clear
That this was on the Buddha's mind (what a word to use
In this connection!) And like a tree with every leaf of different
Color is the blazing tree of meditation. Checking oneself
Is a kind of meditation. Monkey, monk and layman consciously
At all times look within—not much difference, only means and
    manners.
And the mind is controlled by one part watching the action without
When it is taking place. This fatal step without—intended?
Not intended? for pride? for some consideration of another
Cause? or purposeless fidgeting leading up to violence?
My thought—the quickened breath—the mounting pride—
Are these my own? or am I a puppet pulled by strings?
And is the puller of the strings a stranger known by my name
To be discarded? Pride—anger—attachment—aversion—hate
When these ghosts are noticed then they disappear uncherished
When really seen in naked light as corpses long decayed.

Mandalas have their uses also, and can redirect the fever
Of imagination. In the Tantric school the meditating one
Becomes the unreal object of his thought. The raging goddess
Consumes and is consumed. The snake end hair and living
Yellow teeth which decaying crush the bones of my beloved
While all arms thrash and a billion bony fingers claw
The normal state of life and death is too disgusting.
This helps some—perhaps not all—to see the Nothingness
Within the horror and whatever there is busy, real, and
Breaking up the lower nature. Obviously there are many
Kinds of shadows in a single wood. Better yet for some
To be transformed into some tinted Buddha picture for awhile

Serenely sitting chorten-like without abode and solid light
Radiant in the whiteness of the thought. He forgets
His dwelling. Five senses concentrate with open eyes.
Mandala castle is an island of the quiet ocean and in no
Time no clock strikes nor hour passes nor minute ticks.

        Thus non-self: an illustration.

But speaking from the vulgar Western corner of the room
While there is a lot to nothingness, this non-self doctrine
Is too easily proven. What is it that Tibetans do at funerals?
Hacking up the corpse with the bloody chunks ignored
On high and distant rocks, or the funeral pyre ashes
In the river—if there is a river and the astrologer says O.K.
Or maybe common burial like from the funeral parlor
With the windows sealed. Formaldehyde sweet in the nostrils
Of the mourner. Satin softly but uncozy. And the dry
Monotonous drone of Psalm 23. One would expect
That out of boredom the corpse would resurrect and run
Away. The non-self needs no witnesses. Nothing loud to cheer
Or cause excitement joyful. That part of Buddhadharma
Leaves us cold as the slender fingers of the hands unmoving
Of one's beloved. Oh, one rests on unbecoming satin
White and sad beyond the tears, and I see nothing enlightened.
Sorry, a polite digression to add a little pleasant touch
Of graveyard humor. . . . Meanwhile, back to metaphysics.

The Dalai Lama turning abruptly questioning, Are you
  seeing the physical self or the internal self? Answer!

What is the nature of the Dalai Lama? too hard! What is
the nature of a table? Its material, color, size, texture,
And name. Are you satisfied? No need to list the qualities,
some good, some bad. Anyway, the qualities and
That on which the qualities depend. Dependence on each
other and something more of nothingness. Empty
In themselves are qualities. Likewise the Dalai Lama.
What is the Silence within? What is the something extra
Beyond summation of every quality in everyone and everywhere?

THE FARTHER SHORE

Gate, gate, pāragate, pārasaṁgate, bodhi svāhā!
Beyond the Farther Shore, Tathāgata—Thus gone!
Thus come! (however one may translate, no matter,
For coming in and going out is a dubious swinging
Door; although that is what most interests us.
No doors here anyway. Thus come! Thus gone!)
Howsoever, by skillful means we actually stand
Upon the precipice and outward gaze. We stand
Upon the very edge and wonder in the swirling
Mist reflected in the squinting eye. Outside
The mountains tower, yet they are crossed by roads
And armies. Only this precipice filled with surging
Typhoon oceans red weeping sullen while the grey mist
Drifts barely touching insubstantial filaments on
Surf. A Mongol princess draws her silken peacock
Scarf across the ignorant helmet face of a sleeping
Warlord husband. This chasm filled with red battalions:

Māra howling in drunken pleasure at the yellowed tooth,
Unfertile scalp, hardening brain, and much formaldehyde
While even sandal perfume falters. The Farther Shore
Undefined by things is much more flashing radiant
Than any doctrine of non-self, no-thing. Far beyond
The self, beyond the thing, O Bodhisattva!—a raft
A vehicle, a cart, a bridge—the Farther Shore beyond.
Gate, gate, pāragate, pārasaṁgate. This is a quote,
Oh, Zen-like freely, but in desperation. *Bodhi-svāhā!*

THE NEARER SHORE

Yet the one-sided mind has its way and power flows
From the barrel of a gun as our most effective totem
In this era has declared. Why bother with religion?
Why such fragmentation? What is good and evil? Frothy matters!
Since righteous indignation answers every argument
And at Party Headquarters are determined all the rights of man.
No prophet needed. Certainly no nation filled with holy fools.
Right and wrong is settled vivisectionally in army offices or
Bureaucratic palaces reminiscent of an ancient culture
On broad boulevards flags waving. Why do the new ones look like
concrete functional ugly? Anyway, a new washing machine,
Dead peppy government T.V., and a fat belly, Oh America!
Is all that is required of a man, is all that is required.
Plus of course the guns to back them up and someone really good
To hate. We do not play the game as well as those our Slavic
Friends and Asiatic brothers, but we are learning fast.
We are a people quick to learn.

"Your Excellency:
Today groaning under an intolerable burden of terror
And tyranny. . . .As Your Excellency is no doubt
Aware. . . .The situation has now become a grim tragedy.
Hundreds arriving in India and Nepal to escape from
Merciless persecution and inhuman treatment. But
There are thousands of others who find it impossible
To seek asylum in the neighboring countries and are,
Thereby, threatened with immediate death and destruction.
I felt most strongly that something must be done
Must be done immediately to save the lives of innocent
Men, women, and children, and have accordingly sought
The assistance and support of the governments of
Member States of the United Nations. . . .etc. . . .etc. . . ."

I remain,

The Dalai Lama

Oh thank you, Member Nations. Thank you, Thank you
Comrade buddies. Thank you, Mr. Nehru, for thinking
The convenient. Oh, Mr. Zorin, we never will forget that
Movie villain smile. Returned to the once warm Motherland
For the sacrifice of liberation. And the gentle Buddhadharma
Quite dissolved. It is a dream painted in mist on flowing
Water. . . . But why be surprised? Time to wake up to. . . .
And so it goes!. . . . The management grieves at this digression.

33

The Dalai Lama's temple

THE PRAYER

"All you Tathāgatas, Buddhas of the past,
present and future, your spiritual sons and disciples,
who are members of a limitless ocean
of attributes of perfection
who consider all sentient beings
as your only sons. . . .
Let the immense power of mercy arise
and quickly stop the flow of blood and tears. . . .
Our compassion goes to those who destroy
both themselves and others.
Help those rough and cruel ones
to gain the eye of wisdom that discriminates. . . .
Help them gain loving-kindness and a pitying mind."
Thus the Dalai Lama, for we choose among the hours
The one we think the finest. "Father, forgive. . . ."
Echoes of a blessing which absolves. But, Oh! when
Is the sunrise of the pitying mind?

THE HIGHER NATURE

Remaining the Dalai Lama for a moment more or so
The sky already filled with stars, but unless one is
The Dalai Lama political questions cannot help but rage—
And so he talked of meditation. Know first non-self
And with open eyes concentrated on the mandala, absorb
The power of the imagined truth more potent than ordinary
Three-dimensional things. Gradually senses running down
Unwind, decrease in function, and the mind is very still.
Do you see the physical self or the internal self? Two creatures

In a mountain room and many shadows on the mist without
But quieting within. The physical self is not me, I quote
the Dalai Lama
Speaking of himself which is no-self. What is the nature
Of the Dalai Lama?—Never mind, consider still this table.
The ancient argument known in part to Plato. Quibbling
Of Nāgasena. Its material, color, size, and shape; its function;
The qualities and that on which the qualities depend.
What is the something extra besides the full summation? All
These parts! Where is the realness of the table?—a heap
Of wood, a basket full of splinters, a universe of molecules
And dancing atoms. And between the atoms and the flashing
Impulse (so very like a thought) and splitting this and splitting
That and we cannot find a table. Never mind the Dalai Lama,
What is a table? what is a thing? what is? what. . . .
It has no nature other than the Void. There is nothing
Which does not rest upon the Nothing, and the Nothing
Rests upon the nothing. And the Absolute is relative.
A hall of flashing mirrors is the Absolute described
But considered as beyond description is something void instead.
Likewise the human being we investigate and we cannot find
A man, but only Higher Nature. This Emptiness we share
With tables. Far beyond the physical, the nerves and mind —
Still, go deeper and past the bounds of finite consciousness
To the Undescribed the Buddha knew and playfully described.
Turn the thought beyond the thought, into the Emptiness venture
And let the potential kindness wash the shores of twisted half
Crab shapes and cutting shells quite clean. For a moment goodness
Feeble staggers through misapprehension of the Higher Nature
But beyond is the Emptiness which is too full for any picture.

Some kind of Oneness, a shimmering Constellation
Of glittering sparkling points star consciousness within
The Whole. And the overreaching Infinite Mind beyond mind
The Not-to-be-named without finite error or even conceived
In mortality. That, too, alive beyond the sum of parts
Beautiful-Into-Infinity. The Cosmic Breath, the Self
Within the lesser self, the little man within the eye—
All images true and false, yet lacking in the Splendor
Of all things reconciled in gentle radiance. Glowing
Lovely, touching every point of starlight glittering
In perfection. The Garuda and the Snake in peace.
The tiny creatures huddled soft beneath moist leaves
Crawling along green stems. Eater and the jungle eaten,
The discerning mind and the quiet mountain resting
In the peaceful dark. Centuries of past and future
World systems unbeguiled. Dynamically at rest
No consciousness ever lost, rather regained and
Multiplied according to the whim and taste. Beauty
Absolute of the many and the One beyond the wars
Of subject versus object now at peace, at last alive.

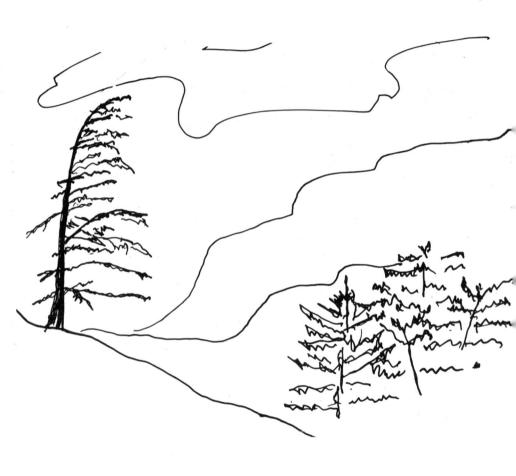

Walk to the village

WALK TO THE VILLAGE

So the interview is over. After all the expectation now
A pleasant "Namaste," and so Goodbye until another
Incarnation. Passing through the open door already
I am another being, so this theory runs. Every moment
Fractured moment brings something new which is the same.
The monk I greet upon the stairs—a yellow butterfly
Robes flapping, is the aggregate of this and that
I met before, yet quite different in this other moment
Lost before I notice it. What will he have to say? this
Impetus of silence. Across the flagstone courtyard
Is the temple. There the Buddha image peers in pleasant
Shadows through the open door into the mountain mist
And far beyond, no doubt, above my cross-legged image
Resting there. In retrospect this twisted question of Tibet
Will be a perfect image, too, proving something dubious
Yet conclusive, about those arbitrary boundary lines
Of any country. About non-violence and the other cheek
Turning to destruction. About the cheerful lovely children
Supremely lucky in their mountain isolation. Tranquility
Still is not forever lost. The remnant will have to change
Somewhat, recognize the turnings of the wheel, and its mis-
Turning, and yet continue living in a host of lands and races.
The Dharma feeble sinks and cannot even hold its ruins
But strangely resurrects in curious places like,
Oh, say—a tourist. The Buddha looks unmoved beyond
The Dalai Lama's throne, and on his right an image
Of the Lotus Born frowning bronzely in the Tantric
Darkness of the corner. Even he—so wildly fierce, is gathered
Here, another refugee. And after awhile the younger lamas

Of the school—real children these, in red monastic robes
Which do not hide their playful spirit—bounce about
The empty temple on their way to class. Quietness,
No talking here, but exuberance of the child is not suppressed
And as they pay respect to those various holy symbols
A playground atmosphere, and even sliding sandals
Swift across the polished temple floor, gliding not
Sedately, because of too much fun, converging puppy pack
In play, yet still they sound like clouds. No melancholy
Here. And off to class to hear the learned lamas teach
Of reassuring Emptiness which is a kindly laughter.
A little way along the path the chorten laughing still
And the moment is too precious for regret. Past the huddled
Stores and inoffensive human apparitions and to our friend
The mist again along the mountain path down to the lower
Town. . . . By then exhilaration quite torrential. . . .the rain
Refreshing like the Raincloud in the Lotus Sutra splashing.

WHITE LOTUS

These symbols are a curious lot,
a shorthand language, and a cryptic
code, to tell meanings, dreams, and
wishes which lie beyond the roofing
of the mind. White lotus spreads
green flat leaves upon the surface
of the pond, absorbs such sunlight
as she may, and lies quiescent gleaming
shell-like still and radiant pearl—
a lotus colored moon. Something eerie
in white stillness, in her blossoms
and her buds, something friendly and
inhuman, quite unfeared by darting dots
and slippery movements in the pond.
Her roots in mud, in inoffensive slime
her gracious stem a cordial welcome
beckons, the floating leaf a steady
platform of stability for certain tiny
creatures, while the blossom petals
quietly unlock to form an ancient mudra—
something pleasant concerning something
pleasant. Unfurled lotus bravely sings
up dark strength within that ever fertile
muck, and with the sun breaks and bursts
into an offering of beauty indescribable
and free—freely given to a moon or holy
stranger quite engrossed in meditation or
to a frog or fly or bug or fish or anyone.

41

Nālāgiri.

NĀLĀGIRI'S TESTIMONY

**(Based on the Jātaka story of the drunken elephant
sent to kill the Buddha.)**

He came down the forest road dust
burdened, heat laddened, with few not
many disciples and all nondescript
in proud rags of humility. Paradox
of no particular interest or meaning
to the cruel men who were my keepers,
Where are they now? nor to me drunk
with poisons that I never know when
jungle wild. The agitated brain within
more filled with fire than all the heat
without. A placid nature twisted raw
meat mean and torn, I do not recognize
myself in memory and yet I bear some
blame for befuddled fiercely staggering
down dusty village streets towards the
river. Nālāgiri, wildest in captivity,
imprisoned in dragging chains, loosed
for an errand that the cousin wanted
—to kill a Buddha or a Child or Man
walking unsuspecting to the town,
it was all the same to me. Cruelty
I can hardly now remember, nastiness
was like the food of yesterday. Who
now distinguishes between the bales
of grass and hay for very·long? but
how important at the time! Regret

for the man dangling from a twirling
trunk, child beneath the foot, woman
hanging there impaled upon the tusk
red dripping in indifferent ordinary
cruelty. People on the high balconies
watched with sympathy and some with
hidden satisfaction, and of all I tortured
I tortured most myself. Without warning
an abrupt corner and there the silly
quite bedraggled beggars. To Devadatta,
to my guards, to those who watched in
hypnotic fascination, he did not seem
a prince, a sage, a god, or anything
but flesh to tear and trample. So they
prodded me with iron spears, screamed,
jumped back, and waited. But to me
a pillar flaming and the fire gentle
and the heat was kindness. He stood,
he loved, the power of his concentrated
thought falling a refreshing monsoon
rain, a cool and shaded pleasant grove
in an empty desert place, a gesture
mild to soothe and heal, a greeting
not of master but of friend, in urgent
asking that I should know him as my
brother. Why! of course I knelt, all
passion gone, insanity dispersed, the
stupid dream resolved, and for once
I was myself—elephant before a Buddha!

and afterwards, although it was their
turn to beat and torture, they soon gave
up, poor victims, and I was sent again
to forest and to field. There unmolested
until the day Māra came to ridicule my life.
How long ago and yet that pillar burns
in odd and unsuspected hearts of many
elephants and some few men. . . . . .*Svāhā!*

VULTURE AT THE TOWER OF SILENCE

It is only a job after all, like any other
job, and one gets used to all its features.
The sinister silence, the isolation ominous
(so they say), are all quite pleasant, indeed
quite relaxing to the troubled mind and
satisfy more appetites than one. Gruesome
is as meets the eye, and when I was young—
very young in other lives, it seemed to me
to be an unkind pleasant thing. Nonetheless
I did my share and generously a little more
and extra to bring some pain into the world:
so what I do now is a kind of added service
making up for much. This convenient blissful
lack of memory does not disturb our dedication.
We stand upon a shape of man, talons firm,
wings flapping, burrowing deep, sharp,
final. Bird noises reassure, we do our
job. Suppose we had a strike or slowdown,
worked according only to the rules, but no!
—no agitators here, serene philosophers of
death. Birds of dignity, serving others' needs,
oblivious to the horror. Quite indifferent.

THE BUDDHA'S FEET

Here now the Buddha's feet, the gabbling guide declared; Come and see the Buddha's feet, the advertisements read—"lotus blossoms springing up where the Holy One did walk," the original impression- the sacred marks of heel and arch and toes, all symmetrical, tidy and quite neat. The imprint burnt on solid stone. Heat-filled blistering solid material in the sun subdivided to infinity comes to naught, gives way before the breath-like touch and slightest thought of his suggested step. As a blotter sucking up a liquid fills, the solid stone is thirsty for the holy impress and sacred picture. But the only trouble is a prima facie doubt and puzzle: these feet, you know, about two feet in length and wider than an elephant foot! his sandal size was surely out of stock. Of course he walked a lot, just thinking of it makes us ache—the palace halls, the palacial mountain pass, the overheated plains. It is a long road from feminine and perfumed gardens through the tangled jungles of disease, old age and death to his friends in old Vārānasī (not so short a hike, especially in the wrong direction). And from there to still another sacred river and on to that cool befriending tree where Māra waits. Those aching feet and pain-filled everything in heat, but the woman gave him curds and milk. And afterwards the Enlightenment business fast concluded, and all the mysteries figured, so his monks have said, he kept on walking. The mixed up route from Bodhgayā to the brows- ing deer in that far-away and famous park and on to all those heathen places with the sacred names. At Śrāvastī Anāthapiṇḍaka was very kind, and from holy Śankisya the man awake took a brief excursion to a minor heaven where his mother dwelt. Then all that back and forth across the Ganges, to Vaiśālī which he liked so

47

much and past the halls of Pātaliputra not yet built, and on to Kusinagara ("Ānanda, 0 do not weep, for all that is born with itself carries seeds of dissolution.")—what kind of a town is that nothing town for a Buddha soon to die! no matter, any place will do. But all that walking—even to the Vulture Peak every day walking down and walking up to bathe and pass poor Bimbisara's jail—he had better feet than anyone we know. Restless, seeking, beyond desire on the move and walking hard to teach—he needed the biggest, kindest, strongest feet. Who in this tired life can keep in step, 0 Ānanda, who?

And yet when the pilgrim treads the marble causeway to a temple in a lotus pond and reverences the foot prints of Mahāvīra—they are the feet of a little child, scarcely more than infant size, tiny, white, innocent, not strong at all. And perhaps this, too, has some hidden holy meaning?

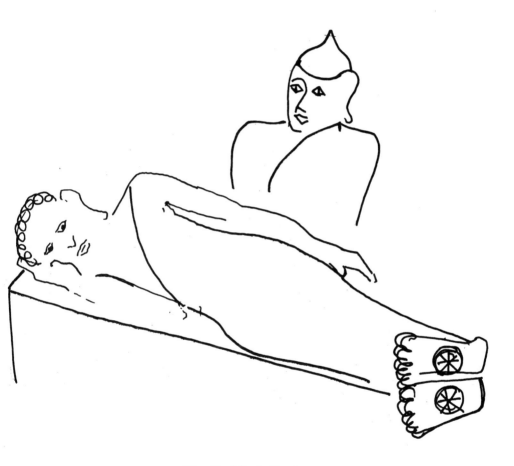

The Buddha's Feet

FESTIVAL OF MAITREYA
THE COMING BUDDHA

He comes, they always say, and yet
We have a way of waiting; Maitreya
Does not seem to hurry, perhaps
Because the night is not quite dark.
More disaster needed. Much more war.
The blood must flow in stagnant
Flooded rivers. And anyway, more death
And more desire. Even the best of peace
Is still disaster in the Bodhisattva's view
And in the bliss wherein he waits, the sight
Of reeking earth repels. The dwindling
Law of inner peace, the tranquil mind,
The love of every creature yet remains
A muddled jungle playground where emotions
Claw and tear without regard. Still
The Bodhisattva waits a settling of the storm:
The pool must quiet and the jungle rest
Before his golden feet step gently down
Upon the lotus flower of the heart. Tibetan
Trumpets blow and cymbals clash metalic
To the whining of a syrup chant which draws
Our plight to his attention. Enlightened one,
Any Being made of light is helpless
For he only helps us help ourselves.
And for that. . .ah, well, there are many eons
And much waiting. Do not hurry, O Maitreya!

Labsum Shedrub Ling

Dragons

TIBETAN DRAGONS

My Tibetan friend who is a Lama says
that dragons really do exist. We do not
see them because a certain well-known
blindness prevents our seeing almost
everything. But they are there. When
the sky is very blue and the clouds
are full and heavy, drifting layer over
layer, serenely gliding, changing into
many shapes and forms as if for pleasure:
one can glimpse a dragon then. Or if
as in a Chinese painting of a storm,
the dark clouds pile and tumble, thunder
menaces, and a knife of lightning tears
apart the sky, sometimes there comes
a momentary kind of second sight. In
heavy rain a splashing tail, the fish-like
scales, the serpent's coiling solidness,
the fringe and mane, the flat and giant
head. He grins and glowers for a instant.

We look again, he is not there. Śākyamuni
once was King of Snakes. All Buddhas are
the friends of dragons, as of all the nāga
people. And the Wisdom Sutras once were
hidden in the rivers underground a secret
in the care of water dragons. No wonder
then that dragons live a life apart as
creatures of the sky who have no time for
sorrow. They do not look for profit and
desire. Fiercely in the joy they revel,
like their friend the King of Snakes.

THE GOD OF LONGEVITY

Gnarled as the twisted branch.
Grey as the mist rising ghostly
between the peaks in mountain rain.
Cool as the raindrops on the lotus
leaf. Clear-eyed as buzzing dot-like
creatures of the insect world who dart
across my lovely Green Slime Pond.

Power of my claw-like hand and mind
clutches the sacred walking stick
whose dragon head speaks and laughs
with me sometimes and then again
at me. Ju-i provides my every wish
with satisfaction, but for tantalizing
youth. Peaches of Immortality somewhere
lie around within the darkness of my cave.
Behind the magic of that mirror, I think
—the one that tells the sadness of the
past and unhappy memories still to come.
So I think, but no matter. Forgetfulness
is easy now. Revered by men who estimate
the largeness of my head to contain the.
vital essence—and so·it does, and more
—much else besides. Within this smooth
cranium lies too little wisdom, and one
small boy running, leaping, beating
against the wall of bone. Only the animals
understand I am not old, but only am,
while now and again I reach straining
my fingertips beyond all barriers
of youth and age and sometimes
barely touch. Bless you and long
life—if that is what you pray.

                                    Taipei

DEER IN NARA PARK

I think they rest, these deer, between one life
and then another. After a row of lives—not good
but far beyond the average, and before another set
of lives to which good karma takes them. Bovine
uncomplicated eye, an honest independent look,
quite unashamed to beg from tourist or from saint
—free of all discrimination, as the sutras say.
Tame, unrestrained, sauntering through the greenest
fields and forests, relaxed beside a Shrine, or if
by chance, a Temple. No dogma and no pride. Happy
to rummage in anybody's garbage can: Thus Nirvāṇa—
wherever one may be, wherever one may really be.
And when bemused they drift across a public road
frenzy comes to a screeching halt, as if the furry
deer were like those sacred cows who stray and are
content in stiffling hells of traffic. Such little
deer do not even face the problems of the quiet cow.
Śākyamuni was their friend not long ago—as world cycles
go, not so long ago; and so they may be pampered just
a little while. And then, no doubt, the nap time
finished, they face another set of lives and do good
deeds and do bad deeds. Their fortunes fluctuate, they
rise, they fall, they fight, they grasp, they question
and object, know the tedium and the pain: they suffer.
But now they rest beneath the pines in pleasant
shadows and in a coolness like the tranquil mind.

ENJŌ-JI
(A Temple near Nara)

Invitation by a friend to sense a Temple,
to feel, absorb, to let flow through. To
unimpeded drift and wonder soft bemused.
Mountain country road winds gentle green
through forest shadows and there the Temple
stands serene at least a thousand years
away. Some pines and shrubs, an overgrown
and ancient pond, hagi, lilies, moss, lichen,
many small flowers and bugs asserting vital
self. Cicadas insistent sing. A second
world in the dark reflections of the pond
and deep below the teeming life of water
creatures.

    Across a curving crescent moon
somewhat bridge shaped and up some steps and
on another plane the dateless gate massive
soaring brown and grey, polished by the years
of cleansing storm, purified of painted triviality.
Surrounded by a school of several low disciple
buildings the Temple quiet in its restful grove.
Stone lantern fireless burning bright. Broad
roof sweeping generous in hot sun, the grey
tiles glint, and within white walls the shade
invites.

As the sight becomes accustomed
to the darkness several Buddhas and their
gentle friends are towering present. They
rest in welcome. Beneath a canopy of golden
curtains Amida comes in view from some far
galactic Paradise, and where he is, the sutras
say, is Pure Land. Merciful Kannons drift
in great abundance here. Jizō haunts the
shadows of dark corners. The great Prince
Shōtoku as a child. Kōbō Daishi holds the
double vajra, and various sacred images and
saints abound. In the corner of a shadow
the Buddha Dainichi upon a golden lotus, his
hands in esoteric mudra placed, and the black
image once gold painted still thinly veiled
with gleaming patches. Strangely familiar,
humanly inhuman, abstractedly alert, introverted
looking out. The suggestion of a smile, no more,
for what he knows cannot be said. One sits
on heels and waits.

Music of cicadas, tree frogs
and such, occasionally a bright bird sings flower
blossoming a somewhat gay and melancholy song.
The great bell sounds again. Vibrations shudder
mellow throb and ripple in the valley. One
merely waits. Then after certain formal prayers
and phrases, the stillness starts. Cicadas sing
in stillness, all sounds flow, the images, ornaments,
pillars and all things flow in perfect stillness.

They are what they are and as they are, yet so much
more. Beyond all tiny concepts of the one, the
sacred Emptiness is full. Dainichi dreams his
dreams in expectation of our odd awakening.
The silence calls for us. Light beckons.

2.

Problems of goodness arise. Problems seeped
in pain. Problems of torment and of anguish
cooking on the fire. Live questions of right
and wrong quivering in the stew. Questions
knife sharp cutting edge slash and destroy.
Nothing seems to happen without multiplication
of no meaning—all that I have brought upon myself
or others, and the very dubious gifts which others
sometime bring—it has meaning to them or me
or someone or not, and politely this is called
free will. But besides and vastly more important
that which the Buddhas bring or not (or use what
ever other name you choose). Out of the context
of the Beyond come startling gifts rich in meaning
but sometimes hard enough to understand. In time
we understand or not, or perhaps the meaning is
out of time, as well as out of tune with my own
wishes. I do not understand when tender things
are lost. What is the meaning of this? What is?

A Buddha

59

Goodness is like the air we breathe
We cannot live without it, but
We do not live for it. A stairway
Only is ethics, a ladder to climb to
Religion, but not Religion. A gate
To the Beyond, an arrow, a feeble
Faltering step towards transcendence.
No more than a glimpse beyond and
Certain it is no cause for pride
Just to be good. And quite disastrous
When offensively dull, for one must
Then raise the question, What *is*
Good? If the grey dust of duty
Is all that men call good, What
Do we seek? And the Buddhas answer
Simple crisp, A perfect consistency
Of means and end, not possible
Now, but worthy of the striving,
And the end of strife a certain
Wisdom which is beauty, radiance,
Splendor, to which no words apply,
Especially "dull". Call of a loon
Perhaps, a mountain path through
Pines, the sun rising above deep
Waters, wild birds singing, or
A lightly falling rain, somewhat
Apply as the speech of the living
Silence. Or perhaps some kindness
Or softly whispered wordless gesture.

A flicker of heat lightning in summer
night is the life of non-man and man as
we know him. Man the inadequate species
all pretence, no need to argue hopefully
expecting very much and everything. What
else is ancient? Some illusion drives us on!

3.

I do not suppose that many foreigners come to this place, but then, we are all foreigners here. Waiting for a passport, for a visa to be stamped, waiting that we may enter where we are and be exactly where we are. Arduous journey distant to oneself, lengthy, dangerous, and brigands haunt the way. False guides, much flattering deception. Lies! But here we really are. This Pure Land which is precisely where we are along the way, and are; although of course the distant goal is not yet reached, it is too close, too near, too now. The Temple here is a little resting place exactly centered where we are, where we started, and where the journey takes us. A pool of silence, a bubbling spring of quiet, a waterfall. To learn a beautiful new language, to see with other than the eye, to really look and know somewhat and be perhaps. No hurry, foreigners are always rushing when they should wait. Listening, waiting, stillness centered. The quickest way is not to hurry.

4.

Problems of mythology and legend
a time bomb blast of discriminating reason.
After all, I am a foreigner and a friend
of Aristotle and Aquinas, and in my day
built cities out of reason. But this is
a vacation now from the finitude of human
thinking, the imprisoning cube, clash
of wheels and gears, sound management
and dollar signs. A criminal escaped
and in hiding here, seeking refuge, lost,
running from the demons, finding peaceful
sanctuary in some reflections of a timeless
past more vibrant real than many multitudes
of prisons. Past reason intuition soars,
and in the hallowed quiet this sacred pantheon
of Buddhas cast a friendly shadow on the
polished floor. Many will say they do not
exist. How quickly they clamor to agree!
First to admit their nothingness. Totally
void, they surely do not exist any more
than my friend and I exist, but perhaps
just as much or more. Modestly they insist
that they are *not,* but nonetheless here is
a Presence comfortable for a stranger to be
near. Friendlier to me, at least, than I am
myself, and I am very grateful. Where I
really am, there I exist. Where they really
are, there they exist; yet neither exist
in any ordinary sense. Let's be daring,

out of existence, really be, then see what
happens. Headed in this Temple by Amida,
this pantheon of friends is full in fact
and implication. Many representations here
of enlightened Beings, and where a statue,
picture, shrine or symbol missing stands,
so much the better still! All the more room
for others, for those ghostly images motions
signs signified so well in absence only. Thus
the facts, and thus kindly implications light
rain girlish fall, lovingly upon the pilgrim.

5.

No need to face any problem now. I turn my attention to Amida.
Namu Amida Butsu!—the ancient essence of the prayer. His fixed
abode is Sukhavati, there he rests and never leaves, so it is not sur-
prising to find him here and there and everywhere. Especially here
in the stillness beyond the incense cloud, within the candle flame,
throughout the prayer. How many aeons past did he take the
famous vow? Koṭis of billions of aeons multiplied to infinity and
very distant, but no matter, it was today and here. Achieving Bodhi
he journied to the Pure Land of his creation and opening to the
fullest the gates of generous mind flung wide he welcomes. The gem
filled land of perfumed waters, the breeze which whispers sounds
of dharma, the jeweled umbrellas, cheerful flags and banners richly
wrought, and best of all, the lotus pond before the Bodhisattva's
palace. Before this rich and humble dwelling of the mind, the my-
riads who have called upon his name. Pilgrims of Samsara on giant
lotus blossoms insect rest. The restlessness is stilled, eager in con-
tentment, alert at ease, their last incarnate life so-called, those

blessed ones who almost know the secret Amitābha tells. He does not speak, but in contemplation there and here he sits, himself a lotus quiet in a radiant foliage halo like a flame of peace, and somehow speaks. Almost one can catch the words, and the meaning does not seem too hard to understand until we ask the meaning. All these ancient problems about self-help and being helped become a little silly in the face of no discrimination. Of course he helps, love is wisdom flowing free, and what saint does not help crushed and bruised. A Buddha of the Gate, golden Amida puts together unrelated flashes of perception and makes a jeweled mosaic. Beyond the Gate is Pure Land where those within the lotus look beyond that Pure Land to where they are and want to be. Amida's call is silent eloquence.

6.

Slim graceful Kannon of multiple heads
in her crown and mind. Her garments fall
in gentle folds. Her delicate hands mudra
teaching peace and calm. Her half-closed eyes,
the softly smiling lips, the middle eye, the
curving Buddha ears almost shoulder touching.
Peace and understanding. Two way peace—
above, below, in various dimensions deep, vast
reaching without limit. Multiple forms
of understanding for multiple pains multiple
souls multiple truths and everything less
than truth in multiple variety. She does
not judge! The total compassion of the

Bodhisattva perhaps is understood only
in receiving undeserved, it applies to all,
lifting the hordes in various dim life stations
of this and other worlds, every creature's thirst.
Thundering judgement, wrath is no help for one
habitually far less than best, but the feminine
hand, the curving graceful fingers, simply caress
and touch and comfort. Dream precise, rainbow
shadow, a fragmentary wisp of understanding, whose
presence prompts a wish to give, forget the self,
and live for at least another. Like any woman
she wins by love and in vulnerability succeeds.
There are many Kannons for multiple creatures
in multiple needs, but I think that all Kannons
are Yumetagae—beautiful creatures of dreams
who change our dreams, as regal Prince Shōtoku
knew. Between nightmare terror and the one
who dreams he dreams, she gently glides, dispels,
transforms, renews, and decorates. A nightmare
is clothed in beauty for a time, and also life
which is another kind of dream no different
than the other. The greater dream to her is just
a winding path through mountain forest after rain,
and she makes it pleasant as herself, nice to be
there, a smiling place, a picnic and a green tree.
Greatly loved Kannon, change our dreams
to quietness, to peace, and make us gentle.

7.

But in the corner of the Temple, the quietest corner in the stillness resting, there in the shadows humbly at one side, is Dainichi, the mind behind the dream changing Kannon, the thought behind the generous Paradise inviting Buddha of the West: unobtrusive, hidden, ancient as the origin, new as the ending of any world or any weary galaxy which wills its own explosion. Curious esoteric mudra: he grasps a finger to symbolize a one of which a one is still a symbol; and there flickers on unmoving lips the shadow of a smile, and half closed eyes glint in alert quiescence. Fearfully still, friendly beyond friendliness and in the realm of awe, it happens that his statue once gold plated has somehow shed its film of wealth. Appearing darkly present now, patches here and there of golden lichen decorate the sacred image in quite uncalculated patterns, a golden dream; but Dainichi is no dream or image. The dreamer of the dream looks far beyond the dream. Answers obvious to questions unresolved call out, but they are too loud for us to hear. A smile frightens. Peace trembles. Sound of quiet is the medium of the answer, vigorous singing effortless and terrible in the still deep pool of Vairocana's presence. They say we are his thought. Dream of existence as real as any solid dream almost. He is thought beyond thought, mind beyond mind, joy beyond pleasure, and dream, if you will, beyond dream. Substantial Emptiness. The Mahayana teaches an identity of Wisdom and Compassion, means and end are one, properly understood, and thus making plausible the famous paradox, Nirvāṇa *is* Samsara: in a way, it is Samsara—properly understood (which is not at all easy to understand exactly, as I know understanding), yet only the real is real; and in a way, of course, it is really not exact to say Samsara, not exactly; that is, because Samsara is not exactly understood. In a way, it is far easier, pleasant, and more natural to understand Nirvāṇa—the coolness, bliss, still clarity, and joy; freedom, and the fulness of potentiality, the unlimited poetry of Sunyata; because all finitude and limitation —illness, old age, and death, to name Shaka's example of a long and happy life—all frustration, smallness, weakness, pettiness, and evil, and the temporal sadness which must always follow getting what we want, somehow nature is curiously unnatural. We never are at home in hospitals, tombs, killings, and sights of suffering disturb even at a distance. Killing is life, so the problem is Samsara, not Nirvāṇa—cool bliss much too obvious and too lovely to be any kind of problem. But then why does Dainichi dream? What is the substance beyond the golden flecks of fading gilt? Why does he smile softly in quietness abounding, dancing, leaping, rapids flowing into corners of the mind and of the heart? Beauty is his thought, the means the end, Wisdom is Compassion, and only dreams are true, and one encompassing fanciful and color dream alone. Five fingers clutch the one. The digits that constitute that posturing ego find the peaceful one. The foolish aggregates of limitation, imagining that they are somehow real, now seek resolution and are blessed with freedom from themselves. They rejoin the flowing dream they only dreamed they left. Welcome of that living stillness quiet flows while Dainichi watches.

Beyond is

8.

A blinding blazing light. Beyond is.
Shade cool restful shadows merge and
part. Beyond is. Snow clouds roll
in above the mountains. Anticipation
of the storm. Then snow begins to fall.
Heavy flakes. Quietly and gentle. Beyond
is. Here is enervating heat, relaxed and
somewhat limp. Palms, bougainvillaea,
oleander, conspiracy to sleep. Beyond is.
Children play and laugh. Fireworks
delight them and they clap their hands.
The night is friendly. Moon explodes.
Beyond is. Lovers meet and plan and
hope. Poetry of schemes to know and see
another. Faithfulness. Beyond is.
Sounds of woodland music. Rustling
leaves, symphony of bugs and toads,
frogs and birds join in. The deep bell
sounds and richly vibrates. Beyond is.
To Vulture Peak the Buddhas come. Creatures
of the light, beyond the light, in the deep
light, enlightened, lightened. Beyond is.

9.

Curious what one thinks seated in a dark corner, shifting from heels to cross-legged traditional poses, then sprawling as if a pool of water poured upon the floor. It is so foreign to be at home. To be, in fact, is to be a stranger in a distant land and when one comes home an oddly far near place to which he journies. The familiar language new, and the scenery most unusual. All the beloved cozy corners painted different. A music somewhat strange. In one of the Upanishads after, I think, some hard saying about the many and the one—"*neti, neti*"— as if anyone dared to speak or remain silent in such a circumstance, or as if anything could be or not, some poor fool (maybe myself in another time and color, or maybe my friend, or anyone) is cruelly asked the very question of which the answer is trumpeted impossible to say. Since he cannot answer, his head falls off. Comic? or not so comic? or a Zen sermon out of time and out of place and out of taste? The Buddha Śākyamuni was more gentle, a polite and gracious host on Vulture Peak. "Thus have I heard" that there is *nothing* to hear, and the hearing is all *music*. Suitable to a Śākya prince, this mountain throne, appropriate to his manner and his taste. A refinement of which a manner is a mirror. Often such and other mountains have been most unkind, but this mountain is a laughing dog, a magic carpet, and a soaring bird. The Buddha is a dragon prince twisted serpentine around the highest peak and grinning at the silly story about the severed head. Galaxies of Buddha fields respond.

On Vulture Peak in deep abyss uplifted
Celeste tinkling expansively hypnotic
calling lost for a beginning or an end
to cheer and comfort. Only Buddhas
can stand that dreadful sight for which
we hanker. Bleakness of the pure.
Inhumanity of the beyond good. Infinity
a cheap and tawdry symbol. Eternity
a geegaw and a little word. These problems
of too much beauty bring to tears, they
acclimatize, sensitize, and dehumanize.
Nothing of worth in Nirvāṇa, in a way,
and nothing of worth is ever lost, so
humanity easily may be traded with some
difficulty. Thus we are told, and that
turning Wheel of Dharma is a living charm
in the hands of a magician who transports
some fool beyond desire to the land of
heart's desire. "Thus have I heard."
Moons planets stars galaxies and other dust
upon the mind swirling veer to Vulture Peak.
A vast assembly of monks free of all depravity,
Arhats like great elephants, disciples famous
for unpronounceable names, royal Bodhisattvas
and Tathagatas from every world dimension.
Much like the gathering of celestial beings in
this deserted Temple which is so small as never
to be filled. The lotus words the Buddha speaks
are most polite and kind. Even the severed head
is made quite right. He does not abuse, torment,
or judge, for he is still a Bodhisattva and a prince.

EPILOGUE

Many versions of the Buddha-dharma with numerous contradictions that all ring true. In this particular Temple mythology is generous, jungle luxuriant and abundant, so there is a place for any odd symbol like myself, my friend, or anyone. We can be at home comfortable, and keep our heads as long as they are any use. It would be lonesome here without Amida. Too severe without Kannon. And Dainichi ever darkly smiling centered. The poetry perhaps is not the final statement, but the final statement is not less and poetry for some is indispensable. Since there is no time, there is time for everything. If there is a sense in which duality is left behind, there is another sense of things no different in which non-duality is a polished floor of beauty on which reflections walk. A rippling pool where insects dart. A sky for soaring birds. A cherry tree in blossom. Clouds above a lovely garden in the rain. A path for pilgrims on a distant journey and a friendly inn. Waiting, I fall asleep upon the porch and cause much comment; but what can they expect? If there is no one here, there is here a place for everyone.

DR. SUZUKI FEEDS HIS CATS

Dr. Suzuki feeds his cats. Kimono clad
he steps into slippers by a sliding door
of his little house. In the garden carefully
walled, his favorite trees and shrubs,
a certain set of roughly textured rocks,
his pond, the lotus pads, and a lantern
hewn of stone. Tantalizing bits of fish,
too bad these fish must die. Apologies
are much in order, but not from cats.
Odd karma to be a cat, not too bad that
life and not too long, but you cannot
stop them stealing fish. Other lives for
that, and the fish, too, must find another
path. Ah well, little enough distinction
between a fish and cat or
between them
and Dr. Suzuki. On a certain plane
no discrimination, they are exactly what
they are exactly, no duality. Old man
stiff kneels, calls his pets by name,
divides the fish, and rises looking far
beyond the eager cats, the fish, beyond.
"Who is to say I am not in Nirvāṇa now?"

Friend

FRIENDS

Cluster of turtles in the sun
Occasionally shift, rest in stupor
Grey rock warm to the touch and
Some lazy fish ripples in the pond
Long legged insects shoot across
The water while dragon fly darts and dips
Dusty are the shrubs and trees
The sky light blue luminous
Bright cheerful and cloud masses
Form regroup reshape effortless
In slow patterns
Children in the sleepy park feeding pigeons
Golden carp lifts his head above the water
Sinks and disappears. FRIENDS here
Dog ambling stretches out and sniffs
Friends the turtle the rock grass
Ripple bugs and growing things and blue
Friends the children birds
Dog carp and more than friends in
Absence of discrimination while
Within the Temple all the Buddhas

Tō-ji, Kyoto

Cryptomeria softly greets the wind with gentle courtesy while other trees and bushes bow according to their rank and station. Moss covered steps descend between the rows of lanterns. No light in these just now, but dignity of stone to match the polished wood within the Temple gates. Resonance deep throated of a bell calls our attention to the Deity within. Within the Temple, within the forest, and within the heart of man and beast and tree. No controversy now, 0 Saichō, for enemies and friends are mutually at rest. And what remains does not remain, and still does neither stay nor go nor in between, and yet there is a Presence. How many soaring birds have spent a life upon this holy hill? How many shy tense forms and startled creatures dart between the leaves and grass? How many troubled men have come here to light a candle, put some incense on the fire, said some words, and gone? Each important to himself and to those whose love has touched him. So the wheel still turns, odd that this is so. But the one who is a memory, what has he now found? What is glimpsed between the stars? What says the sea? the wind? the bird? the heart? How speak the grains of dust within the Buddha's palm? That beyond illusion is a dream, and beyond a dream are endless shining rows of dreams like lanterns on the steps; and at the heart is Peace. But Who dreams? Who dares to ask? and Why? Now beyond questions, 0 Saichō, do not rest in peace: Live on in peace! And bless all living creatures if you may.

Enryaku-ji

TEMPLES OF KŌYA-SAN

ARRIVAL

Unique advantage of the mountains is
that one looks out and there is sky. Not
ant-like looking up and twisting, simply
looking straight ahead and there is blue
with drifting clouds and stars and moon.
And there beyond the daytime blue and there
beyond the nighttime mystery, infinity is.
At a glance. An advantage over urban living.

****

ROOM

In a world of sliding panels, a golden screen,
a teakwood table very low, and in a niche a
hanging scroll with matching flowers, it is easier
to cleanse the mind than in many other places.
To kneel upon tatami mats, sip tea, politely
wait and gently speak, or no words at all are
needed, only listen to the wind in pines and rain.

****

MORNING

Very early in the morning light rain falls in
pleasant mist. Perfect harmony of little shrubs
and trees and rocks. Green leaves moist glisten
smoothly fresh in sunshine. Red, orange, purple,
all flowers awake. There is sound of bells
and chanting in a darkened corner beyond some
rich and golden panels, something about soaring cranes
who glide above great pines. Cryptomaria
cast a thousand spires to a pearl grey sky.
Buddhas smile. A bullfrog croaks. It rains.

****

GARDEN

How many times have I sat upon the steps in
this little garden? Rested upon the polished wood?
Admired the screens and panels? Seen familiar pictures
of snow upon pine boughs—the same ducks splashing
in that pond—mountain peaks beyond golden mist—those
gibbons chattering in the trees—the flowers—the
tiny bugs—all friendly creatures and familiar?
How many times have I looked out at this garden
and with the wind, or as the wind, drifted through the needles
of the trees—touched upon flamboyant
brilliant flowers brushed by the quivering leaves
—skimmed across the pond—and greeted brothers
of the water and the woods, and somehow could not stay?

MUSEUM

What would you say of a museum where
people remove their shoes before they enter?
Walk upon tatami mats in solemn softness? There
is a hush as if within a Temple and
visitors pause in reverence before symbols
of the known, unknown, and loved—at once
such symbols have these aspects quietly polite.
On tattered scrolls some very ancient Buddhas
look from realms both far away and here and now.
In bamboo groves the heron and the swan, in
tiny ponds some ducks and fish, and on mandalas
large as rugs the mystery hangs unhurried in the
stillness until someone hears the path. In a
special place the ritual instruments of Kōbō
Daishi, his calligraphy, his alms bowl and
sandals. And in the hall of statues the many
Buddhas, Bodhisattvas, Arhats, learners, students
and their friends look down unworried by delay.
Shaka's blessing gesture is of peace. Amida
comes. Jizō throws his cord to save a creature.
In fierce good humor Fudō stamps upon the lower nature. Dainichi
grins and knows whatever that may be which only Buddhas know.
And in this pleasant place, before each symbol, sign and
painting, at the foot of every statue and along
each picture frame, a gleaming row of silver coins.

****

79

The Buddhas of the Gate rest in lotus posture
within their minds, and in the shadows wait
bemused. The mist of pungent incense burns, and
one old woman bows hands together, lights
a candle, kneels and mutters. The golden statues
watch. The Buddha of the Gate of form and shape
and sometime splendor observes the tired shoulders, the
wrinkled skin, the moistened eye, and ancient
age. The Buddha of the Gate of feeling notes the
signs of passion long since spent, the hopes
and scars, frustrations long dispersed, a certain core of
sweetness of a young and happy girl. The Buddha
of the Gate who glues together all impressions firm
in an order never clearly stated and yet somewhat
understood, sees the dull mind, the locked doors
of memory, a lost quickness of the thought, alert
and questioning perception dissipated for this life,
and full regret. The Buddha of the Gate of all past
and present karma casts a glance along an endless
corridor of lives, while unspent karma swirls fog
like in dusty nooks and halls, relentlessly demanding.
Serenely then he looks ahead to still another row
of lives, a fiercely endless chain of galaxies, and
forbids in mercy bittersweet remembrance or a vision
of the future. The Buddha of the Central Gate who
is pure Mind which is No Mind understands the words
she does not say and cannot now remember, for within
his thought is every thought and within his mind is
every mind. Smilingly he treasures that pathetic

burning candle, the sweet incense glowing at his feet,
the folded hands, the weary form before him, some heaps
of this and that, and so he blesses. All of the Buddhas
agree within, they nod but do not move, they speak but
do not verbalize, they smile, they see the aged figure
shortly young and new again, and much they do not say. But
then again they look within, they contemplate
beyond all Gates. What could be within the Gates?

****

SHINNOIN

Chinese style: a grey long building, matching
wings, on the fourth side a wall and heavy gate.
Beside the gate a large bronze bell moss-fringed.
The middle building filled with tiny rooms and
sliding doors and panels. Many gold decorations
from very ancient times. Pictures of famous holy
men, some trees and ponds, several soaring cranes,
some sassy ducks, snow upon pine boughs, sacred
gibbons in the trees. Another building for the
guests, and across the courtyard is the Temple.
In the empty yard a few small pines, little shrubs,
unsymmetric border tortured rocks of doubtful shape.
The courtyard there of gravel newly raked in certain
patterns. No monks. Quiet, motionless, and void,
the moon sheds golden radiance. More splendid far
than indoor treasure. Glowing soft and living, awful
Light. Who can endure such beauty? Bright melancholic
night of weeping, fear, regret, and beauty. Cold mist.
Cold Mountain mist.
Mountain Cold Mountain. Mountain
mist. Cold Mountain. Much too close and closer coming.

****

Endless stone walk through the vast
cemetery to the tomb where Kōbō Daishi
lives. Many famous piles of ashes rest
along the way. Square cenotaphs and
curious pillars with the square, globe,
ring, triangle, crescent shapes that
show the whole of things. Moss and
lichen, broken hearts, and the mountain
wind to sweep away the smell of death
The mighty trunks of ageless cedars lift
their swaying lovely branches to the wind,
the sun, the fire, the moon, the storm,
and in peaceful shadows down below we
pilgrims creep. We stumble up the path,
a jagged line of drunken ants. Drifting
dusty world, indifferent fresh and tearful
rain. Each drop a tear, each tear a prayer.
By temples ringed, and then by trees, within
the center Kōbō Daishi here is known to rest
in deepest meditation. Unsleeping saint, not
dead, within an unconditioned realm he lives.
A thousand lanterns gleam before his shrine.
Incense clouds petition rise. A tide of softly
sad and murmured prayer rushes fiercely to the
silent tomb. Hearts of anguish and troubled
minds of men are ever in abundance here. Bless,
Kōbō Daishi, bless. He does bless everyone,
no doubt; and yet the smallest Buddha knows

the answer is self-knowledge. Kōbō Daishi
gently blesses nonetheless, and waits. Waits.
Miroku yet must come. Waits until relationships
are placed in certain order. Waits until a
holy saint may leave his tomb unquestioned.
Waits until suffering is a shadow and forgotten
fancy. Waits. Kūkai will have no pilgrims
then. And in some golden stupa in a cloudless
sky and peace and boundless blue. But now.

****

WALKING HOME

A bell somewhere in the distance sounds
deep and dark and vibrant, and somewhere
men are chanting. Somewhere in a storm
of ringing gongs and clashing cymbals the
incense rises with our prayers. The Buddha
Dainichi dreams of these our bells and gongs
and cymbals. He is amused there are so
many. He glances at a fly, a bird, a man.

****

PUZZLE

A jagged rock, grey and speckled
as if with age, stands in
the wet garden
unperturbed by rain. The fierce storm
beats against the stone, rain pellets bounce
away or melt absorbed within the moss.

****

MU-TEI

Zen pattern. Mandala universe in one small
garden. Sun brightness blinding gravel heat
to burn the self away. Cicadas insist they
are alive and much important. Beyond the low
clay wall with rippling ocean tiles cedars
pines bamboo and maple, and within the narrow
garden a few rocks. Famous rocks. Scattered
haphazardly with intense deliberation. Carefully
by chance. All these words and theories—
a group of mountain islands in the sea, mountain
tops above the clouds, tigress carrying cubs
across a stream: what could not be true beyond
conventional sight? Yet looking closely tight
shut eyes, maybe five galaxies of giant size
drifting through a sea of chilling space. Gigantic
each and tiny, of many parts and vast and small,
each almost infinite in life insistence. Only
five universes here, but just outside the map,
no end. And in another way these rocks and
gravel combed in pretty patterns are just that.

Ryōan-ji

Tigress carrying cubs (Tārā)

HEAVY SNOW

Heavy snow upon the mountains. The pass
is blocked and we are locked within. Forest
strangely white and crisp beneath a darkened
sky. The cedars and the pines bend branches
low under the weight of whiteness. Animals,
birds, fish, and insect creatures, are hidden
in their cozy places. The Temple roof covered
white. Breaking a path between the trees,
across an open space of perfect stillness,
three pilgrims walk, holding red umbrellas,
past stone lanterns almost covered by the
snow. This quiet world of untouched snow
could be another galaxy of momentary calm
which never ends. It could be, it is another
world, and one well known within the shelter
of the Temple. They say more snow will come
tonight. White world in deepening peace.

Kōya--san

SNOW FALLING

Snow falling breathless gentle no words:
It only is. The forest still. No pilgrims
now, no path. An open space between tall
trees. Out of dark clouds waiting patiently
for a giant golden brush to trace some sacred
character no one can read. A rice paper
street unmarked. All shapes now
blurred dim dark cream light drifting snow. Stone
lanterns almost hidden. Mounting tiers
of the great pagoda layered white like
some tremendous Buddha birthday cake. It
is somewhat reminiscent of the mountains
where he lived, but much more gentle soaring.
Golden ornament of the peak still hopeful
pointing although the sky is heavy grey.
The bells on the corner of each tier
silent. A silent hush awesome dread-filled
speaking terrible wonderful. The snow still
falls and whiteness everywhere white quiet.

A COVERED MIRROR

A covered mirror is very Japanese
and wise. A slim reflecting glass
dares the hand to lift a red and
gold brocaded curtain. It does not
pay to look too close and see oneself
on ordinary days. What is gained by
too much knowing? arrogance and pride,
vanity and shame, regret and maybe
tears. And it is quite dangerous
to look too deep within that mirror,
for the Kami of the little mirror
knows the Kami of the Bead, the Sword,
the Greater Mirror none may see.
She knows the Sun, the Fire, the Light,
and so much more. One might fall
within that mirror, or be stricken
by a Face who looks without into the
false and lesser world which is my
home. A Face so beautiful that one
might die from so much beauty. And
if the mirror is not covered, none
can tell who watches as he moves about
the room. Better lift the brocade
just when necessary, only at the special
times, in a manner slow and gentle and
perfectly correct, very careful and polite.

                    Isé

Tori

IN DEDICATION AND ENVY
OF ARIWARA-NO-NARIHIRA

Except for being handsome, rich, and young
and famous—envy of every man and the idol
of every woman, like the dreams of everyone
we know—except for this strange and freakish
karma quickly spent, I suspect that Ariwara-
no-Narihira was in his heart much like the rest
of troubled men. A flood of passion clashes
with a flood of tears and Narihira is cast out
upon some bleak and joyless rocky beach which
has a name that only demons know. Mind destroying
tumbling sea and grief within not greeting, not
anything so definite as a clue. Merging storms
become a double headed monster to tear Narihira
to shreds to claw devour vomit. He is very polite,
this Narihira, and he bows so very low and charming
while from his smile the soft vocabulary of the
court sweetly river flows in gentle murmur. Every
gracious gesture and each soft and sweetened word
is a kind of symbol of despair. What else is new?
Any child of woman knows the same: the love of
which he writes is an ocean with no shore, a sky
without a port, a chilling rain, and a storm which
sweeps away the quiet mind—a friendly monster
poking in a garbage can to eat tranquility then
                    beluga belch

HIS JOY

A simple open meeting and look of revelation,
no deceit. The gentle smile unforced, laughing
eyes of no pretense, a rippling whisper of a
word, and softer still, the pose relaxed and
unashamed. Narihira knew those moments which
jewel-like fringe the greater moment of the
present. Within that hallowed ritual of a new
discovery there existed no abuse in him nor any
triumph, but grateful taking as he gave. Home
before the ancient symbol of the one, his body,
mind and heart at one, he gave without a question
and fluently could practice that even greater art
to peacefully receive. And in the tortured realm
of multiplicity so endlessly dividing still he
sought the one, and within the seeking barely
glimpsed a moment undivided. A moment pure, how
shall we say?—as fresh cool water bubbling in
a mountain stream—as the spacious welcoming and
undivided sky—as the unconfined and drifting
cloud—as the butterfly fluttering without a
sound from leaf to leaf. There was no dishonesty
until he donned his clothes and mask, and said

     "My name is Narihira."

HIS GRIEF

A momentary dream may contain more reality
than the ordinary so-called real. With fingertips
we sometimes touch the most elusive truth, and
then, no more!—even as we watch, it fades away
in mist and there is nothing left—save to weep
and wonder. We have walked softly in the path
between the pines in heavy pouring rain. Strained
our vision watching holy lips, waiting tensely
patient while the statue speaks in silence. Climbed
the sacred hill, observed the drifting cloud-like
message in some foreign tongue of which we do not
even know the name, much less the grammar. Sought
to know another, and then, like mist we cannot grasp,
it all dissolves. It all becomes a dream more real
than truth. A memory more real than real. A sadness
and a melancholy cruel as hot sunshine on the parched
and thirsting earth. The vision hardens while the
memory burns. We cry in desolation because that we
knew so well we cannot grasp, we cannot touch again
nor have nor hold. A sad farewell, and common.

HIS SECOND THOUGHTS

If not in this, then in another life let us walk
awhile together. If not in this, then in another
life, let us promise faithfulness. A fresh, new
start, no deceit nor complications, and we will know
each other in the honesty—the clear uncomplicated
look—the undeceitful glance—the truly friendly word
—the smile. We will speak words which will ring
familiar echoes, for we have spoken tender words
in so many lives before, and will again. Patience!
the mysterious chances, the singing overtones, those
understandings unexplained, the kindness and the joy,
the changes on the chimes: these the clues conclusive.

A SHINTO SHRINE

In the forest
at the end of twisting gravel
many paths
behind a curtain
a locked door
beyond an outer building
and a yard of stones
and then another fence
bars across the gates
another building tightly locked
another fence
across the courtyard
another door
more locks and bolts
    And there the Shrine
    thatched roof and
        ridge of crossed
        and golden beams
Behind more doors and locks
    in a secret cabinet within
    which no man sees:
        There the Kami.

Outside the little families clap their hands and bow, whisper something silent; the hens peak in the gravel and the rooster proudly struts; in a tiny booth black hair falls on white blouses and girls with long red skirts and silver ornaments sell pretty picture postcards of the place. They are polite and smile.

NOT HAPPY SHRINE

There is a shrine which bothers me.
I cannot quite explain a certain hill
which rises stable solid rock. The hill
itself is pleasant, covered richly green,
all the many trees and bushes one expects,
all the grasses, ferns and flowers. One
crack there, a crevice glimpse into the
inside of the hill. Maybe four feet wide
maybe thirty feet or more in depth moist
black troublesome. It has never known
the light of day of moon of stars of even
darkness of the night. It has its own
nighttime. Deep within the hole there is
a narrow tori pressed together out of
shape of the usual polished wood, curtain
and behind the curtain something red—
a lantern? candle? or something in the
troubled mind? Unflickering spot of red
in a nightmare from which one cannot
awaken. This is a shrine from which
I quickly walked away, but which I cannot
manage yet to leave. Who built it? when?
and why.................................?

SHOES

These racks of shoes outside
the Temple—man's pair of very
polished Western shoes, scuffed
up sandals, children's shoes,
tennis shoes, plastic slippers,
shoes that have no tops, shoes
lacking sides, some shoes with
worn out soles, some tourist
shoes, and other shoes with heels
and open toes for ladies of high
fashion. So many shoes for a
little Temple, so many styles,
so many needs. No doubt as many
styles of prayer to go with all
these shoes. Gods must weary
of these shoes, perhaps their
reason they withdraw. Back home
in Church it seems so rude to
wear such shoes, so undressed up.

THE TOMB AT SIKANDRA

Some ninety odd names of God gleam in moonlight
As a touch of night caresses gold and precious ornament
To cool the marble tomb. But deep below the true
Tomb lies—marked in darkness only by the nothingness
Of sleep unbroken. Catacomb crude walls without
A mark of hope or peace or rest or patience, while within
The unmarked pit and beneath a marble catafalque
The Emperor is outstretched. Weep, O beloved wives!
O daughters, weep! O sons! O concubines! Wail and weep!
Nearby the favorite horse never to be mounted nor
The friendly hand upon the mane. Not far the beloved
Elephant also rests and the trunk does not lift nor
The familiar piercing screech of triumph sound. Weep!
O horse! Weep, O elephant! O monkeys, weep! Let all
Deer and wild things wail! And those who did debate
so laughingly and glib, let their hearts be broken now!
Truth cannot help you now, for the Chosen One of God
Has ceased to listen. The Emperor sleeps and does not
                    Wake!
                                        Agra

98

SIGHTSEEING IN A TEMPLE
AND FORMER COURT OF KINGS

Vast structure for the comfort of the gods
inspires respect, wonder, questions plentiful
of issues now too tiresome to relate—
all the wearisome tribulation of beast
and man and bird. The play of gods?
or problems for the gods to solve and heal?

Vast structure for the comfort of the kings,
their court, women, visitors, elephants and oxen
is deserted now. Only cooing pigeons, some cawing
Indian crows, and small chipmonks who dart
where courtiers softly stamped. Kings are gone,
birds and animals are much at home and gods remain.

At the core of history is the sadness falling
dust film heavy upon the evil and the good.
Not for us to judge these men who cannot now
argue any case or justify their deeds. Only
for us to bless the living and the dead with
liberality marked by sorrow, changing, shared.

In the rooms behind the Swarga Klasam, where
the king would sit in glory, are women's quarters.
Soft graceful glances and a creature in a sari
more colorful than birds, a whisper shimmering,
jewels and bangles, heat—I look again, a chipmonk
flees. Unforgotten laughter ripples in the empty room.

Tirumala Nayak,

Madurai

99

A PERSONAL NOTE

Of all the friendly animals and birds
My totem is the dog. Eagerness to please,
no deceit and somewhat shy, cowardly but
brave in desperation, loyal and completely
loving without a thought of consequence—
such are all my dogs. No happier sound
than thumping tail. No greater eloquence
than red moist tongue and loving liquid
eyes. Not all the bodhisattvas take exotic
shape. Indeed, true friends. They know,
they do not verbalize but only know who
is their friend. There have been so many.
Farm dogs whose names are long forgotten.
City dogs whose memory marks the stages
of my life. Some more aristocratic than
their master, but only kindness counts with
them. No dog ever claimed a pedigree, only
silly owners. Some were waifs and very glad
to find a home. All enjoyed comfort. That
spaniel, black and silky hair, soft and tender
look, and eager face. Another little dog,
white and brown, lost and starving at my gate.
Not long to live and make my home her home
and make me welcome there. And my old friend
too smart to be a dog—the hostile poodle,
giant, black—a large stuffed toy the children
thought until he told them quickly otherwise.

He knew his own and simply did not care
for any other. Even yet I grieve at the
thought of these and others. And my present
mongrel dogs are truly children of the streets,
but loved and loving like some royal child.
One is jealous and possessive black, exclusive
deep and.grasping love. Another skittish, yet
she always comes unless she's called. Louise
and Gina are good names for these. And Suzy is a
happy girl, the prettiest one, with her feelings
much too easily hurt. And George, largest,
strongest, bravest, is one important dog;
pathetically he needs to be important, and in
his little world he is just that. God bless
all my dogs of past and present, and may we
have a rowdy, noisy meeting in some better place.
God bless all dogs, keep them secure, and bring
them safely home to shelter. God must love dogs.

Personal friend

EAST AND WEST

A living creature in a net should be the emblem
of the world. Multiple forms of poisoned bait which
few resist, full anodyne of love and total antidote to
prayer. And now the East, the legendary land of holy
men and lovers, chews upon the bait and feels the
hook within. She has her business men and comrades
and cries aloud in pain for things. Ancient temples
quiet wait and deep within the shadow'd halls some aging
men and women, and perchance a couple young and new who
at that sacred moment are too enthralled to think of
things. The holy beggar long since lost his way, and
wanders in the forest, if at all, yet gods still watch
bemused and tender. So the East obtains precisely what
she wants. She achieves the endless sorrow of possessing
many things. And in the West, so joyless and so rich,
owning all those things which no one needs but wants,
full fighting busy all the while, thrashing in the net,
and thinking that is peace. In the West a few young people
stop and wonder, along with others not so young, who reach
and clutch those sparkling jewels the East has thrown
away. So the wheel turns and karma has its way again,
and it could be someday that the West may be new rich
with meditation, give birth to saints and sacred lovers,
prize the poetry of prayer and deep devotion, and rest
in stillness and in joy. Then the East could have
her things until someday again the wheel reverses.

Bodhgayā

THOU

Thou of many masks, all things and every creature;
That greater shining Person; radiant true Unperson
surpassing every name and indication; Kindness quick
rushing to the cry of pathos; Joy beyond the rippling
laughter; listening Ear in every Temple, Church, and
creature's heart: Thou art pure Mercy, and we are
Thine within Thine Heart, and Thou in us. A billion
galaxies of names are not enough, each divine, empty
and quite full. Do mysteries need to be resolved in
this or any life if we only glimpse that Thou which is
so far, yet here? Only sense that Thou within the
swirling mist which drifts across the lotus pond, then
turns to rain. The nameless Thou that men must name.

THOU MASK

Thou, whose mask is the world:
Show us Thy true Face of Love.

Protector

ILLUSTRATIONS
by the author

TITLE	Page